AF270385

Dog Groups

Toy Group

by Julie Murray

Level 1 – Beginning
Short and simple sentences with familiar words or patterns for children who are beginning to understand how letters and sounds go together.

Level 2 – Emerging
Longer words and sentences with more complex language patterns for readers who are practicing common words and letter sounds.

Level 3 – Transitional
More developed language and vocabulary for readers who are becoming more independent.

abdobooks.com

Published by Abdo Zoom, a division of ABDO, PO Box 398166, Minneapolis, Minnesota 55439. Copyright © 2024 by Abdo Consulting Group, Inc. International copyrights reserved in all countries. No part of this book may be reproduced in any form without written permission from the publisher. Dash!™ is a trademark and logo of Abdo Zoom.

Printed in the United States of America, North Mankato, Minnesota.
102023
012024

Photo Credits: Getty Images, Shutterstock
Production Contributors: Jennie Forsberg, Grace Hansen
Design Contributors: Candice Keimig, Neil Klinepier

Library of Congress Control Number: 2023938004

Publisher's Cataloging in Publication Data

Names: Murray, Julie, author.
Title: Toy group / by Julie Murray
Description: Minneapolis, Minnesota : Abdo Zoom, 2024 | Series: Dog groups | Includes online resources and index.
Identifiers: ISBN 9781098284060 (lib. bdg.) | ISBN 9781098284787 (eBook) | ISBN 9781098285142 (Read-to-Me eBook)
Subjects: LCSH: Toy dogs--Juvenile literature. | Dog breeds--Juvenile literature. | Dogs--Juvenile literature. | Dogs--Behavior--Juvenile literature.
Classification: DDC 636.765--dc23

Table of Contents

Toy Group

There are more than 20 dog **breeds** in the Toy Group according to the American Kennel Club (AKC). Each dog is **unique**!

Papillon

Toy dogs are miniature versions of dogs from other groups.

Dogs in the Toy Group were **bred** to be companions. Many are lap dogs.

Yorkshire Terrier

Characteristics

Dogs in the Toy Group are small. Most weigh less than 14 pounds (6.4 kg).

Chihuahua

Toy dogs have surprisingly big personalities. They must be properly trained.

They are intelligent dogs. The Toy Poodle is the smartest.

14

Poodle (Toy)
RUSSIAN TOY
SHIH TZU

Toy dogs do well in smaller homes. This makes them great for apartment living.

Pug

Toy dogs do not need a lot of exercise. However, they do enjoy short walks and play.

Cavalier King
Charles Spaniel

Toy dogs are loving. They need human interaction. They love to be with their owners.
Maltese

More Toy Breeds

Chinese Crested

Havanese

Pekingese

Italian Greyhound

Shih Tzu

Silky Terrier

Glossary

bred – developed over time for a certain purpose.

breed – a particular type of animal.

unique – being the only one of its type.

Index

Online Resources

To learn more about the Toy Group, please visit **abdobooklinks.com** or scan this QR code. These links are routinely monitored and updated to provide the most current information available.